SUPER SKATE[BOARDING]

COMPETITIVE
SKATEBOARDING

rosen publishing's
rosen
central®

New York

HOLLY CEFREY

To Ethan

Published in 2009 by The Rosen Publishing Group, Inc.
29 East 21st Street, New York, NY 10010

Copyright © 2009 by The Rosen Publishing Group, Inc.

First Edition

Library of Congress Cataloging-in-Publication Data

Cefrey, Holly.
Competitive skateboarding / Holly Cefrey.—1st ed.
    p. cm.—(Super skateboarding)
Includes bibliographical references.
ISBN-13: 978-1-4358-5050-7 (library binding)
ISBN-13: 978-1-4358-5394-2 (pbk)
ISBN-13: 978-1-4358-5400-0 (6 pack)
1. Skateboarding—Juvenile literature. 2. Skateboarders—Juvenile literature. I. Title.
GV859.8.C44 2009
796.22—dc22

                                                                2008014949

Manufactured in the United States of America

On the cover: A skater competes with an air-to-fakie.

CONTENTS

INTRODUCTION

A skater rides the rails at the indoor course of Skatepark of Tampa in Tampa, Florida. The park opened in 1993 and has become internationally known.

oug had been skateboarding since he was seven years old. By age thirteen, he had an ease and control on his board that gained him the respect of his friends and local skateboarders. Doug was finally headed to a skateboarding competition—and it was no ordinary competition. He and his dad were going to Tampa Am 2007.

Tampa Am is one of the biggest annual amateur skateboarding competitions in the world. Every year, kids as young as twelve travel to Tampa, Florida, to compete for prizes such as surfboards, travel vouchers, watches, iPods, and trophies. Tampa Am's 2007 competition drew more than two hundred amateur skaters from all over the world. The competition was open to any male and female skaters who were amateurs. More than five hundred skaters apply each year, but only about two hundred are chosen to compete.

On Thursday morning, Doug and his dad went to Skatepark of Tampa (SPoT), where Tampa Am is held every year. Skate parks such as SPoT allow skaters to gather, share tricks, invent new tricks, and hold competitions. SPoT is historic because it has been holding major skating events for fourteen years. Doug was thrilled to be visiting this famous landmark for the first time.

Doug and other skaters took turns warming up during the eleven-hour practice session. The next day, he competed in the street qualifiers. More than one hundred skaters were split into five heats. He competed against twenty-five other skaters in his heat. He was allowed two fifty-second runs, which are single trips along a course or route.

Practice makes perfect. A skater runs the course during warm-up. He'll have a few more passes to try to get the feel of the course before competition starts.

Doug knew that his first run could have gone better. He worked really hard on the second run, doing his coolest tricks and hitting all the obstacles. He qualified within the top sixteen competitors of the day, which meant he made it to the semifinals on Sunday. On Saturday, he and his father watched the second session of street qualifier heats. They wanted to check out the competition. Saturday's top sixteen competitors would also compete in Sunday's semifinals.

Sunday's semifinals started at 11 AM. Only ten winners of the semifinals would advance to the finals, taking place later in the day. Doug had two one-minute runs. He had big air time, noseslides, ollies, and kickflips. He anxiously waited as the rest of the competitors finished their runs. He was thrilled to be competing with the other skaters. They were doing tricks that he was still working on and trying to perfect. One skater even did a new combination, which excited the crowd.

Knowing he was in their league made him beam deep inside with pride. Doug didn't make the finals, but he didn't care. He was having the time of his life. During the finals, a sponsor approached him and his father. "A lot of greats have skated in the Tampa Am, and they didn't even make the semifinals their first time," the sponsor said. "Here's my contact information. Let's talk about your future."

Skateboarding competitions such as the Tampa Am are growing in popularity and size each year. Competitions and events occur at the local, regional, national, and international levels. You don't have to be an older, seasoned skater in order to compete at the national and international levels. Many events offer amateur or hobby-level competitions. This means that you can be skating on the same course that the pros use. Prizes at events range from boards and gear to large cash awards. Whether you are just starting out or are heading to nationals, this book offers practical guidance on what to do and expect.

CHAPTER ONE

STARTING OUT

Team sports are a part of everyone's educational development. Whether you're playing softball, football, basketball, or volleyball, you're required to play sports that involve your peers.

Team sports teach valuable lessons. You learn to work with others. You learn to be patient and to communicate. You learn how to be creative with peers of different skill levels in order to win a game. You learn to make sacrifices for the team, like allowing a teammate to play your favorite position. However, in skateboarding, you yourself are your team.

When you skateboard, you are your own teammate and coach. You develop your own skills, create your own tricks, and decide your plan of attack. You decide where and when to practice and how you want to skate.

Many professional skateboarders say they love the independence that the sport provides. You still learn the same lessons that group sports provide, but in a different way. When you share a course or park with other skaters, you'll learn to be patient and communicate effectively. When you watch other skaters do their stuff, you'll learn how to be creative as well. You may even partner up with some skaters to share resources, tricks, and ideas. While skateboarding is an independent sport, you're never really alone. You're part of a community, but your ability to succeed rests solely on your shoulders.

A skater turns a construction pipe into his own half-pipe. While skating can be done anywhere, wait until you're seasoned and confident on your board to try something like this.

Making a Statement

Skateboarding has been around for about fifty years. Various forms of the skateboard have been around even longer. The skateboard comes from the old days of soapbox carts and scooters. Hobbyists in the early 1900s used ordinary items, junk, or spare parts to create man-powered vehicles. They raced these homemade vehicles for sport. Because there were no motors to power the vehicles, many races took place on hills. Eventually, West Coast surfers and enthusiasts designed what would

Rich Lopez catches big air and the attention of the crowd during the Mountain Dew National Championships of Skateboarding held in New Jersey.

become the modern skateboard. They used small boards with four roller-skate wheels attached to them. On days when the ocean waves were too calm to surf, these people "surfed" in the streets.

Besides surfers, another culture has been closely linked to skateboarding throughout the decades. Teens and young adults who considered themselves outcasts sought skateboarding as an activity. You don't have to fit a certain image in order to be a successful skater. If you're interested in skateboarding, then it really should be about the sport and not about joining a group or wanting to belong. Skateboarding requires highly specialized skills that only you can develop for yourself. How you wear

Public places to skate are becoming more popular. Wide, spread-out parks with a variety of obstacles are one of the best places to practice and gain skills.

your hair and clothes won't affect whether you're a great skater. Only practice will.

Be Safe and Respectful

Society is still warming up to the sport of skateboarding, but fortunately, you can turn to skate parks for immediate acceptance. There, you'll find several communities of skaters that do what they love without being interrupted. Each skate park has its own rules, so follow them for your safety and for everyone else's. You can search for a local skate park

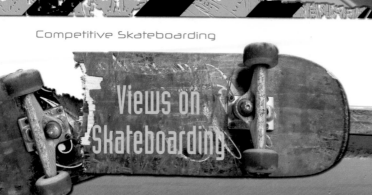

Views on Skateboarding

Skateboarding as a sport has come a long way, but many communities still see it as a threat to safety and normalcy. Many community leaders feel that skateboards are too noisy. They worry that the speed and tricks are too dangerous for skaters and innocent passers-by. Manufacturers have created a variety of anti-skating hardware for towns to use in their parks and streets. These devices prevent skateboarders, bicyclists, and inline skaters from doing tricks. Skaters use benches, planters, steps, handrails, ledges, and curbs for tricks. Park officials put the hardware on these objects so that skaters can't use them as obstacles for tricks.

The GrindMinder is an example of a device that prevents skateboarding. It is a metal sphere that is placed into the cement of curbs and ledges. Several are placed all along the edge. They are spaced every few feet. They make the edge bumpy. Because they are spaced apart, people can still use the bench or ledge for sitting.

A basic grind is when you slide along an object on your trucks rather than your wheels. The trucks are the metal hardware connecting your wheels to your board. Your trucks grind along the curb, bench, rail, or ledge as you move forward.

If a GrindMinder is used, then you won't be able to grind on the object. It's designed to stop you immediately. Skaters have been thrown from their boards when they try to skate where anti-skating devices such as these are in place.

Similar devices in any park, street, or town make a clear statement about skateboarding. It is not welcomed. If you skate in areas with these devices, then be careful. You may get hurt if you ignore the devices and skate there anyway.

Towns with these devices may also have laws against skating. Make sure you know whether you are skating in a place that allows it legally. You'd be surprised where it is and is not allowed. Even Tampa, which eagerly holds the Tampa Am every year, does not allow street skating. It is illegal there, like in many other cities.

by contacting your parks and recreations representative.

If you're using a public park, then be patient and share the space with other skaters. Be especially aware of pedestrians and non-skating park-goers. If you find that a group of skaters is preventing other skaters and park-goers from having fun or feeling safe, then report them immediately to the local park official or police officer. The larger communities of skateboarders are trying to have skateboarding viewed in a more positive light. Dangerous groups such as these are what keep cities from supporting skateboarding projects and events.

Skaters like challenging themselves outside of skate parks. Before doing this, make sure you master the skate park or smaller obstacles first.

At some point while skate-boarding, you'll have to stick up for good values. Be honest and represent your sport well. Patiently reason with anyone who thinks that skating needs to involve aggressive or dangerous behavior toward others. If someone is really aggressive, then walk away. You'll easily find another place to skate in safety and peace. Don't hesitate to report aggressive behavior to a park official or other trusted adult.

Skateboarding is a true sport. Practicing good behavior and respect of the sport is important, especially when you encounter sponsors. Sponsors are individuals or companies that financially support talented athletes. They aren't interested in supporting wild and angry hobbyists. They want to invest in individuals who bring an authentic enthusiasm to the sport. Starting off with the right attitude is a great way to ensure future competitive success.

Be Patient

When first starting out, your urge may be to do tricks of every kind. You might want to do a grind, ollie, nollie, kickflip, or a slide. It's normal to watch the pros and wish you could skate just like them. Just remember that they make it look easy because they've done the tricks hundreds—maybe thousands—of times. At some point, you will get frustrated as you're trying to learn new tricks. It's part of the sport. Professional skaters will tell you that they're good because they never gave up, even when extremely frustrated.

Knee Slide

1. Run up the transition.
2. Near the top, jump and turn around and land back on the ramp with your knees.
3. Slide down the transition.
4. Keep your feet dragging behind you.
5. As you slide, lean back to keep your balance.
6. Once you stop, get back up and begin skating again.

CHAPTER TWO

GEARING UP AND GETTING OUT

As you advance in your skating, you will seem reliable to sponsors if you show that you know your gear. They want to support athletes who can speak intelligently about the sport and its gear.

Skateboarding involves accidents, whether you're a skilled professional or just a beginner. For the first few years of skating, wear as much protection as you can. Wear a helmet and elbow pads. If you're skating on a ramp, then wear knee pads, too. Protect your joints and your head from injury. Get comfortable using a helmet either way because many skate parks and events require that you wear one.

When you fall—and you will fall—try to avoid putting your hands out or continuing into the fall. Try to break the fall by running or walking through the stumble. You may feel that you look funny, but "running off" the fall is a great way to avoid injury. If you're going to hit the ground, then try to fall on your side with your arms at your side. When you hit, roll with the fall. Many skaters break their arms by trying to stop a fall with their hands. If you receive any bruises or sprains from a fall, then have them checked immediately by the skate park medical representative or your school nurse.

In the 2007 X Games, skater Jake Brown fell from 45 feet (13.7 meters) in the air after riding up the ramp. He was able to turn his body so that he would land on his backside. He miraculously walked away from the accident. In an interview with reporter Diane Sawyer, he said he had a lot of time in the air to think about the fall. He considered the best position for impact and positioned his body. He may have saved his own life by knowing how to fall correctly.

When you get your new skateboard, practice your balance by standing on it in the grass. Stand on the board, jump on it, and try to switch your feet without falling off. Try balancing with the front end up, then with the back end up. Try leaning to the left and right without tipping over or falling. You may feel silly, but this activity is strengthening your muscles and skills. When you're learning tricks for the first time, use the grass as well to practice performing them in place. The first few falls will be softer. Then you can take it to the pavement.

Anatomy of Your Board

You don't need to spend a lot of money on your skateboard; just make sure that it's well built. You can go to a skate shop and buy a readymade beginner's board, or you can customize your board. Skateboards have very few parts. Get to know them and become an expert. The little adjustments that you make to the hardware can improve your skating tremendously. Here are the basic components of every skateboard:

- **Deck** Most decks are 7.25 to 8.5 inches (18.4 to 21.6 centimeters) wide by 29 to 33 inches (73.7 to 83.8 cm) long. The front of the deck is the nose. The back is the tail. The nose is typically wider than the tail. Both are typically raised upward for easier tricks.
- **Grip tape** This is a sandpaper-like surface that is applied to the top of the deck for better grip.
- **Trucks** These are the devices that connect the wheels and the deck and are responsible for steering.

The hardware of a skateboard seems straightforward, but even slight adjustments can change the way your board handles. Pictured here is the truck, including the axle, hangar, and kingpin.

- **Base plate** This plastic plate acts as a cushion between the truck and the deck.
- **Axle** This is the rod that connects two wheels to a truck.
- **Hangar** This holds the axle.
- **Kingpin** This is the screw that holds the axle in place. When adjusted, it allows for looser or stiffer steering. When turned tight, the steering is tight. When turned looser, the steering is more flexible.
- **Wheels** Wheels are offered in various sizes and levels of hardness, or durometer. The harder the wheel, the faster it

You should take care of your wheels. They need to be cleaned frequently if you ride in the street. They easily can pick up dirt, glass, and debris. Change them when they become worn.

rolls but the less control and comfort you have. The softer the wheel, the slower it rolls but you don't feel every pebble on the ground.

Starting out, you should opt for a softer wheel. Larger wheels are great for speed. They're usually used for skating on half-pipes. Smaller wheels, since they are lighter and allow you to do ollie tricks more easily, are often used for street skating.

If you find a used board, then make sure that the deck is strong. Many decks break from constant wear and strain. Also, you'll want to know the

Taking Care of Your Board

You don't need the most expensive board and equipment in order to be competitive. You just need to cover the following basics:

- Keep your grip tape clean. Use a vegetable brush to clean it.
- Wash your wheels with mild soap and water. Remove stones and grit with your fingernail or a pair of tweezers.
- Clean your bearings. Bearings are metal casings that attach the wheels to the axle. They help wheels turn. Most bearings today are waterproof and sealed, meaning that water and dirt can't get inside the casing. It's a good idea, though, to keep the outsides clean by removing them from the wheels and wiping them down with soap and water.
- Invest in a pair of skate shoes. They can replace your regular sneakers if you can't afford both. Skate shoes have wider bottoms for better balance. They have thin, gripping soles so that you can "feel" your board better than with regular sneakers. They also have padding on the outside edge to protect them from the grip tape when you ollie.

hardness and size of your wheels. Make sure they are right for the specific skating that you are going to do. Don't skate on any board that isn't put together well. It can lead to costly and painful accidents.

Your Stance

Skateboarding is exciting and seemingly simple. You get on the board and you push yourself with one of your legs, you ride it, and steer. This process, however, is the end result of several sessions of experimentation and practice.

The first step is determining your own natural stance. This is called footedness in board sports. If you aren't comfortable in your stance, then you won't master skateboarding. Just like you write with one hand, left or right, you'll naturally want to push with one leg, left or right. Try riding a skateboard on a flat surface—first with

For the most confident stance, experiment with what feels comfortable. As you master tricks, you may find that being flexible in a variety of stances delivers better results.

your right foot in front, then with your left leg in front. After several tries, your body will tell you which way feels natural.

Riders with their left foot in front have "regular" stances. You'll be pushing with your hind right foot while balancing on your front left leg. Riders with their right foot in front have "goofy" stances. You'll be pushing with your hind left foot and balancing on your right front leg.

Some riders push with their front leg and balance on their hind leg. This is called "mongo" foot. For a strong foundation, practice skating in all stances. While doing this, you'll also be improving your balance, steering, and stopping.

Getting Out There

All professional skaters start from the beginning. They get good at the simple things such as maintaining balance, pushing, riding, steering, and stopping. Many skating tricks combine the basic elements of skating and other tricks. Basics are important to master for competitive skating. You'll want to be able to perform tricks "on the fly," or improvise. Each competition has its own layout of obstacles. It might occur to you that a particular layout would be great for a trick combination. You'll have just the practice session to master that new combo before a competition. If your basic skills are strong, then you'll increase the chances of landing that new combo.

Basic tricks include acid drops, kick turns, slides, truck stands, ollies, 50-50 grinds, and manuals. These tricks, along with others, are done in local and national competitions. Take your practice to the street, park, or skate park where you can be around other skaters. You'll be able to watch more skilled skaters and pick up tips. Find out who skates in local competitions. Watch what they do and keep practicing.

Dropping In

1. Stand at the edge of the obstacle, put the back end of the board against the edge, with your wheels over the edge, against the wall.
2. Stand on the board with your hind foot. Put your weight on this leg while placing your front foot on the board.
3. When you're ready, in one swift motion, push onto the board with your front foot, as if taking a heavy step.
4. Lean forward. This step is key; it pushes the board off of the edge and onto the ramp for fast action!
5. Plant the front wheels firmly on the ramp.
6. Roll to the flat bottom and prepare for your next trick.

CHAPTER THREE

THE COMPETITION CIRCUIT

The best resource you can use when starting out in competition is your local skate shop. Many of these shops sponsor local events and shows. Events usually take place in skate parks in larger communities. Smaller communities may not have skate parks. Events might be held in the parking lot of a shopping mall, school, or church.

Skate shop owners and employees will tell you where to practice and compete if this is the case in your town. Many local skate shops will also sponsor local skaters in bigger competitions. Get to know the skate shop community. Share ideas with them and learn from them. Making friends in this community will help your competitive skating career and may even get you sponsored.

If you don't have a local skate shop, then try to make trips to nearby towns that do. Check out the events that they organize or sponsor. Ask them if they would be willing to help organize an event in your town. Doing so will bring them more customers and stir up more interest in the sport. You can also try organizing an event through your school or church. Talk to your school or church officials about holding a summer event. Invite skaters from neighboring schools and churches to attend. You can ask local restaurants or stores to donate prizes. This is a great way to get support started for a new skateboarding community in your area.

Amateur contests are a great way to show off one's talents. Ten-year-old Morgan Burgess competed in local contests at small parks, such as Baker Bowl Skate Park in Ohio. His skills soon grew noticed in the skating world.

The Skate Community

If you do not have a public skate park, then you can do something about it. There are organizations that can help. The Skate Park Association of the United States of America, or SPAUSA, has been working for more than ten years to support this cause. SPAUSA provides support about safety, fire codes, laws, and other complicated issues. Its Web site offers a step-by-step guide on getting approval for skate parks. You can learn about raising funds and awareness for your cause. The organization will even call your city officials if you need help getting started.

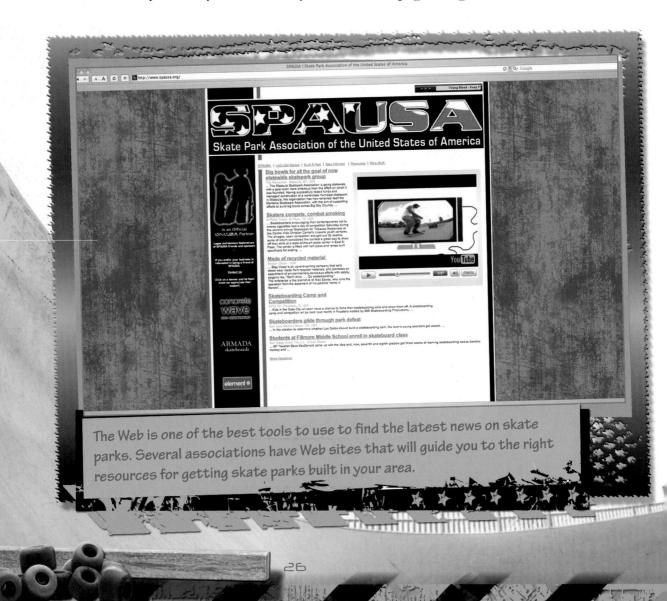

The Web is one of the best tools to use to find the latest news on skate parks. Several associations have Web sites that will guide you to the right resources for getting skate parks built in your area.

You begin by getting your local skate shops, bike shops, and sporting goods stores involved. Give them petitions to sign. They will ask that their customers sign the petition. The people who sign it are showing support for a skate park. Local governments value petitions because they represent what a group of people want. If a large number of people really want a skate park, then your city council is more likely to say yes. At the very least, the council will make plans to include skateboarding features in future public park projects.

Other organizations, like the Tony Hawk Foundation, help build parks in low-income areas. Hawk started the foundation in 2006. He believes that skateboarding is a great activity to keep kids off the streets and out of trouble. The foundation has helped to support more than three hundred national skate

Basic Tricks

Acid drop To skate off of a platform, dropping to the ground.

Grind Sliding the trucks along the edge of an obstacle such as a curb or bench.

Kick turn Balancing on the back wheels while swinging the front of the board to the right or to the left.

Manual Lifting the front wheels off of the ground while rolling.

Ollie Popping the skateboard into the air. The skater "jumps" with the board underneath his or her feet.

Slide Sliding the bottom of the deck on a surface such as a rail.

Truck stand Flipping the board so that the skater stands on one truck with his or her other foot hooked on the other side. The board is almost upright.

park projects. Currently, 180 skate parks have been opened. According to the foundation, about 1.5 million youths are enjoying these parks and staying out of trouble. If you're living in a low-income area, then you can visit the foundation's Web site to learn more about bringing a skate park to your town.

Regional Competitions

If you're competing locally with some success, then the next step is to compete regionally. Regional competition is great for skaters in communities without skate events. Use resources such as the Web to watch regional competitions. Many skaters and event sponsors post their films on sites such as YouTube. You can see the level of competition at the regional level before you even set out on your trip.

Be honest with yourself. If you're not quite at the regional level, then practice in order to get there. Go to your first regional without the expectation to win. Go with the desire to learn instead. Watch the other skaters. Listen to advice. Have fun in your competitive rounds. Don't get too worried if you're not perfect. Pay attention to who sponsors the events. You'll want to approach these companies when you're ready to take the regionals by storm.

Many regionals lead to larger national competitions, like the Free Flow Open. Free Flow Open by AST or Action Sports Tour takes place every year in more than a dozen regions. The 2007 tour took place in seventeen regional areas. These included Utah, Colorado, New Mexico, Tennessee, Ohio, and Pennsylvania. The entrance fee is set very low at the regional events, at around ten dollars. Any skater under the age of eighteen can compete. He or she must be an amateur. The winner of the regional event gets to compete at the national level. The organizers

More national and international competitions are being held now than in previous decades. Events like this one in Australia draw big crowds and eager judges.

pay for the hotel stay and travel to Orlando, Florida, for the regional winners. The tour also offers a Junior Jam Open for skaters under the age of twelve.

Other regional tours and region-based events include the Concrete Rodeo Tour, Grind for Life, Damn Am, and the Mid-Atlantic Skate Series. Participating in any of these events will help you to build your career.

What You Need to Bring

Judges at the Free Flow Open and similar events are looking for specific types of tricks. At the regional level, they don't expect you to skate like a pro yet. They are looking for originality and creativity with your tricks.

Judges look at the individual elements that make up your whole run. Did you use all of the obstacles on the course? What tricks did you do? How many tricks did you do? They'll judge whether your tricks were difficult and original. It's OK if you mess up on one or two because they are looking for a variety of successful tricks over errors.

Judges also look at how you approached your tricks. Did you attack the obstacle with determination? This means, did you go into your trick with focus? If you did a trick but looked like you lucked into it, then it's usually not judged as well as a focused, determined trick. The judges also look at style, or how graceful you are on your board. They'll consider the order of your tricks and your use of the obstacles. They'll think about your run and whether you chose tricks that linked well together. There may be other elements, depending on the event.

Grind

1. Approach the side with speed.
2. Begin to position your body so it's balanced, but be ready to put more weight on your hind foot.
3. Use this weight to force the truck against the edge, with the hind wheels overlapping the lip.
4. The force of speed and gravity will propel you along the lip while your truck grinds the edge.
5. When you're ready to break back, put pressure on the tail and swing your direction back toward the center of the ramp.
6. Regain your balance and ride away.

CHAPTER FOUR

A PRO'S LIFE

There are two main kinds of skating at most pro events. They are street skating and vert (vertical) skating. Vertical skating involves a vert ramp, or a full-size half-pipe. The name "vert" refers to how the curvature of the ramp rises to a vertical angle at the very top. You'll have to decide at some point whether or not you want to compete in one, the other, or both, depending on your expertise.

Events with street skating will have large, open courses with many obstacles. The obstacles are designed to imitate public park structures such as benches and handrails. You're free to attack the entire course any way you like. How you attack the course and the tricks you choose will determine your score. You can perform a combination of fancy "flatground" skating using only the pavement or tricks off of obstacles. It's really up to you how you want to use the course and which tricks to do. However, the most variety often gets the best score.

Vert skating involves vert ramps, which take a special type of nerve. As you "drop in," or enter the ramp coming down from one side, your speed increases. When you come up to the other side, gravity holds you in place and brings you back down. At the tops of both sides of the ramp, you'll do a variety of tricks before coming back down. It's fast paced and challenging. Expect a lot of spills while you're learning. Be patient, too, because when you watch vert pros, you'll see that they still

Skating events are supported by fans but also by big sponsors. Here is an aerial shot of the Globe World Cup Skateboarding course and vert ramp with sponsor logos.

have bad spills, even in competitions. Always wear a helmet and pads when vert skating.

Becoming a Pro

Comparing amateur and pro can be confusing. You can be a pro skater and never leave the regional circuit. You can be an amateur skater at the national level. The main difference between amateurs and pros is that professionals can rely upon their skating for a living. They have won

Your Health

When you're an athlete, you are using your body as a tool. It's only a good tool if it's in good shape. Skateboarding requires a lot of energy. This energy must last over long periods of time. In order to have this energy, you need to treat your body as any athlete should:

- Get plenty of rest. Your body requires sleep to repair itself from the day's use and stress. Sleep and rest allow your body to build its energy for the next day.
- Eat well-balanced meals. Your body will be building energy from food. Eat plenty of vegetables and fruits. You don't have to eat meat, but it is a great supplier of protein. Protein keeps your cells and muscles healthy.
- Add other exercise to your life. Don't rely on the exercise that you get from skateboarding to build and maintain your muscles. Add at least one other form of weekly exercise.

events, which often include large cash prizes. Most pros have sponsorships. They are making enough money that skating can be their only source of income.

When companies sponsor skaters, they often give them free gear such as shoes or decks. In turn, the skater allows the company to attach his or her name to the products. The skater must honor the conditions of the sponsorship. It can be as little as doing a couple of television commercials. Or, it can be as involved as doing several guest appearances throughout the year.

Mid-level skaters can earn between fifty thousand dollars and one hundred thousand dollars a year. Skating champions can make between five hundred thou-sand dollars and one million dollars. Companies that sup-port these athletes aren't just

Events like the Slam City Jam attract pro skaters who give it their all. Both males and females ride hard, pull out big air, and demonstrate high-level tricks.

looking for the best skaters. They are looking for the entire package. They want to know that you love skating—and the fans. They want to know that when you're interviewed, you will represent the sport and the company very well. Do you have a firm understanding and clear enthusiasm for your sport? Do you know who all the great skaters were? Do you pay respect to current great skaters?

Getting Sponsored

The key to getting sponsored is getting involved. Go to as many local, regional, and national events as you can, even if you're not skating. If you can't go, then read skateboarding magazines and watch clips on Web sites. Create a list of sponsors that you like. These will be the companies you approach for sponsorship as your skating gets better and better. Check the companies' Web sites. They may have directions for applying for sponsorship.

Make a video of your coolest tricks. Most sponsors view hundreds of videos a week. Try to put a lot of action in the first thirty seconds of the video. Get right into it and show trick after trick. If you don't have a video camera, then contact film students at your school or local art school. They have to make films for their projects, and skateboarding is a great subject. Tell them you'll "act" for free as long as you can get a great film with tricks edited together. It doesn't have to be fancy; it just has to show your skills.

Send the film to sponsors. If you can send it as a digital file via e-mail or on a CD, then it will really be convenient for them. You can also submit it to YouTube, and then send that link to the company. Keep updating your film as your tricks get better. Don't give up. Someone will at least offer advice on what to do next for your particular situation.

The Pros You Know

The names you may know, like Tony Hawk, Danny Way, and Ryan Sheckler, are familiar because they're pros. They have earned high rankings, fame, and a lot of money. All three have gained respect and sponsorship. All three have won top medals at pro events such as the X Games.

The popularity of the X Games and other pro events is growing every year. The X Games is like the Olympics for extreme sports. Athletes from all over the world come to the annual event to compete in skateboarding, snowboarding, BMX, MotorX, rallying, skiing, snowmobiling, and surfing. Winners get gold, silver, or bronze medals. They also get huge cash prizes, such as fifty thousand dollars.

Other national events include the Tampa Pro (which also offers some events for amateurs). The prize purse includes twenty thousand dollars for first place in street and seven thousand dollars for first place in vert competition. The Slam City Jam offers more than one hundred thousand dollars in cash prizes. First place in street is fifteen thousand dollars. The Action Sports Tour offers the AST Dew Tour. It awards more than one hundred thousand dollars to top finishers individually. Events take place in Maryland, Ohio, Oregon, Utah, and Florida.

The Maloof Money Cup is also a spectacular skateboarding-only event. It awards up to four hundred thousand dollars in cash prizes. The winner of the pro street takes home one hundred thousand dollars. The winner of the pro vert gets seventy-five thousand dollars. The Etnies Goofy versus Regular (GvR) is an event that has teams compete against each other. Goofy-footed and regular-footed pros are invited to compete. It offers seventy-five thousand dollars in cash prizes.

While big money and fame are a reality for pro skaters, it shouldn't be why you want to compete. Most pro skaters will tell you that they didn't become famous because they sought fame. They are where they are because they did what they love. They love skateboarding.

Approach your competitive career with the same love of what you're doing regardless of whether you win or lose. Don't get too upset if you don't get the sponsorship you're hoping for right away. Practice a lot and keep positive. You're never too good to practice. Keep a sharing, open attitude and try to help others gain skills, too. You'll find that the skating community will give back what it gets. Before you know it, doing what you love may take you around the world.

Frontside Air

1. Approach the lip with moderate speed.
2. Shoot past the edge.
3. As you rise, keep your knees bent.
4. Turn your shoulder toward the center of the ramp as you sail through the air. Grab your board as you are turning, to keep it with you.
5. As your body follows through the turn, begin to straighten your legs.
6. Reposition your body so you're ready to ride the ramp back to the center.

GLOSSARY

acid drop To ride off of a short ledge, dropping to the ground.

amateur The level below professional status.

axle The rod that connects two wheels to a truck.

base plate A plastic spacer that goes between the truck and the deck.

city council A group of local government officials that makes decisions on your behalf.

deck Also called a board; the wooden board that a skater stands on.

determination Focus and intent to do something.

footedness How you naturally stand on a board.

grind Sliding the trucks along the edge of an obstacle such as a curb or bench.

grip tape A sandpaper-like surface that is applied to the top of the deck.

hangar Hardware that holds the axle.

improvise To do something without a plan.

kick turn Balancing on the back wheels while swinging the front of the board to the right or left.

kingpin Hardware that, when adjusted, allows for looser or stiffer steering.

manual When the front wheels are lifted off the ground while rolling.

ollie Popping the skateboard into the air. The skater "jumps" with the board underneath his or her feet.

originality A quality of newness.

outcast An individual who lives outside of traditional society and its rules.

petition A paper with signatures on it. The signatures represent approval for an idea.

slide Sliding forward using the deck or the wheels. Also a technique used to brake or stop when using the wheels.

sponsor Individual or company that financially supports talented athletes.

trucks Metal hardware that connect the wheels to a board.

truck stand Flipping the board so the skater stands on one truck with his or her other foot hooked on the other side. The board is almost upright.

vertical Straight up and down.

FOR MORE INFORMATION

All Girl Skate Jam (AGSJ)
Patty Segovia-Krause
2018 Shattuck Avenue, #12
Berkeley, CA 94704
(510) 927-6365
E-mail: patty@allgirlskatejam.com
Web site: http://www.allgirlskatejam.com
The AGSJ organizes pro and amateur events for female skaters. Cash prizes and
    awards are given at several yearly events.

Skateboard Canada and *Skateboard* Magazine
2255 B Queen Street East, Suite 3266
Toronto, ON M4E-1G3
Canada
E-mail: info@sbcskateboard.com
Web site: http://www.sbcskateboard.com
This organization offers an online magazine with articles, information, contests, and
    park listings for skateboarding in Canada.

Skate Park Association of the United States of America (SPAUSA)
2210 Lincoln Boulevard
Venice, CA 90291
(310) 261-2816
Web site: http://www.spausa.org
SPAUSA will help bring skate parks to your hometown. It will also make sure your
    current skate parks offer everything you need to be safe.

Tony Hawk Foundation
1611-A South Melrose Drive, #360
Vista, CA 92081
(760) 477-2479
E-mail: information@tonyhawk.com
Web site: http://www.tonyhawkfoundation.org
This foundation brings skate parks and funding for them to low-income housing
    areas. Its goal is to give youth a place to go and enjoy skating, rather than get
    into trouble on the streets.

Vancouver Skateboard Coalition
c/o Secretary
103-241 St. Andrews Avenue
North Vancouver, BC V7L-3K8
Canada
Web site: http://www.vsbc.ca
This group strives to promote unity among Vancouver's skater community. It also
    works to create safe environments for skaters.

Web Sites

Due to the changing nature of Internet links, Rosen Publishing has
developed an online list of Web sites related to the subject of this book.
This site is updated regularly. Please use this link to access this list:

http://www.rosenlinks.com/ssk/cosk

FOR FURTHER READING

Barwin, Steven. *Sk8er*. Halifax, NS, Canada: Lorimer, James & Company, Limited, 2008.

David, Jack. *Big Air Skateboarding*. Eden Prairie, MN: Bellwether Media, 2007.

Hocking, Justin. *Skate Parks*. New York, NY: Rosen Publishing, 2006.

Junor, Amy. *Skate!* New York, NY: DK Publishing, 2008.

Kelley, K. C. *Skateboard Stars*. Mankato, MN: Child's World, 2007.

McClellan, Ray. *Skateboard Vert*. New York, NY: Scholastic, 2008.

Morris, Neil. *Food for Sports*. Portsmouth, NH: Heinemann, 2006.

Sievert, Terri. *Girls' Skateboarding*. Mankato, MN: Coughlan Publishing, 2007.

Streissguth, Thomas. *Skateboarding Street Style*. Eden Prairie, MN: Bellwether Media, 2008.

BIBLIOGRAPHY

Arkins, Audrey. "Dream Job: Pro Skateboarder." Salary.com, 2001–2005. Retrieved March 1, 2008 (http://www.salary.com/careers/layouthtmls/crel_display_Cat10_Ser176_Par276.html).

Cave, Steve. "How to Clean Skateboard Bearings." About.com. Retrieved March 1, 2008 (http://skateboard.about.com/od/boardmaintenance/ss/HowToCleanBear.htm).

Good Morning America. "Skateboarder Falls 45 Feet, Lives to Talk About It." August 6, 2007. Retrieved March 1, 2008. (http://abcnews.go.com/GMA/ESPNSports/story?id=3447416).

Mullen, Rodney, and Sean Mortimer. *The Mutt: How to Skateboard and Not Kill Yourself*. New York, NY: Harper Collins, 2005.

Riggio, Jay. "Sponsor Me!" EXPN–ESPN, October 14, 2007. Retrieved March 1, 2008. (http://expn.go.com/expn/story?id=3050699).

Skateboard.com. "Trucks." 2008. Retrieved March 1, 2008. (http://www.skateboard.com/p-skbd_101_trucks/index.html?zenid=07lof7ib1c11hiouikftcfsp87).

SPAUSA. "Get a Skatepark in Your Town." Retrieved March 1, 2008 (http://www.spausa.org/first-steps.html).

Thomas, Danny. "Skateboarding Rolls into the London 2012 Games." British Broadcast Corporation, September 26, 2007. Retrieved March 1, 2008. (http://www.bbc.co.uk/norfolk/content/articles/2007/09/05/sport_olympicskateboards_20070905_feature.shtml).

Werner, Doug, and Steve Badillo. *Skateboarding: New Levels—Tips and Tricks for Serious Riders*. Chula Vista, CA: Tracks Publishing 2002.

INDEX

About the Author

Holly Cefrey is an award-winning children's book author. She learned to skateboard from her big brother, Ethan. Both had an active childhood, playing outdoors from dawn until dusk. They rode skateboards, scooters, and minibikes on the neighborhood streets of Louisiana and Nebraska. Always looking for new adventure, she learned to drive three-wheelers while her brother raced karts. Cefrey still loves extreme adventure, but more so now as a spectator.

Photo Credits

Cover (background), p. 1 (background) © www.istockphoto.com/Steven Robertson; cover (right) p. 1 © www.istockphoto.com/AHMAD FAIZAL YAHYA; p. 3 © www.istockphoto.com/Shane White; pp. 4–5 © www.istockphoto.com/Richardson Maneze; pp. 4 (inset), 6 Rob Meronek/Courtesy of Skatepark of Tampa; p. 9 © www.istockphoto.com/Daren Crigler; pp. 10, 25 © AP Images; p. 11 © istockphoto.com/Charles Shapiro; p. 13 © www.istockphoto.com/Bart Sadowski; pp. 15, 23, 31, 39 © Tony Donaldson/Icon SMI/The Rosen Publishing Group; p. 18 © www.istockphoto.com/Brian Finestone; p. 19 © www.istockphoto.com/Bryan Malley; p. 21 © www.istockphoto.com/Michael Svoboda; pp. 29, 33 © Martin Philbey/Zuma Press; p. 35 © Zach Podell/Icon SMI; background and decorative elements © www.istockphoto.com/Dave Long, © www.istockphoto.com/David Kahn, © www.istockphoto.com/Alice Scully; © www.istockphoto.com/Leif Norman, © www.istockphoto.com/Ron Bailey; © www.istockphoto.com/jc559; © www.istockphoto.com/Reid Harrington; © www.istockphoto.com/Lora Clark.

Designer: Nelson Sá; Editor: Nicholas Croce
Photo Researcher: Amy Feinberg